BOSTON'S
FREEDOM TRAIL

BOSTON'S FREEDOM TRAIL

Illustrations by Jack Frost

Text by Robert Booth

The Globe Pequot Press

Chester, Connecticut 06412

Library of Congress Catalogue Number: 81-81853
ISBN: 0-87106-954-7

Printed in the United States of America

First Edition

Cover and book design by Barbara M. Marks

Foreword

For 175 years, the Freedom Trail in Boston was a concept without a name. In 1950, a Boston newspaperman, William G. Schofield, came to the realization that the greatest number of sites sacred to the beginnings of our republic anywhere in the United States were located in Boston, and moreover were all within easy walking distance of each other. Then, in a moment of inspiration he conceived the name, Freedom Trail.

Previously each site had its own organization and its individual idea of how to present itself to the public, and as a result, the planning of an orderly visit was at best, confusing, and the less than studious visitor might easily go away having missed something significant. Now, as the Freedom Trail has brought all of these places together under the aegis of the Freedom Trail Foundation, it is easy for the visitor to get a rounded and balanced view of the historic sites, and through such an experience to enhance his knowledge of American history. Most important, under the confederation which now exists, there is no compromise in the individuality with which each site is presented.

This has been worked out of a period of time, thanks to the efforts of many groups, including the Advertising Club of Boston, the Greater Boston Convention and Tourist Bureau, the Freedom Trail Commission, and most recently the National Park Service, which today plays a vital part in the maintenance and interpretation of the sites along the Trail.

This book is thus intended to present to the reader a package in which you will find admirably described, each of Boston's significant historic places. We of the Freedom Trail Foundation welcome you to our city, and trust that this booklet will help to make your visit both a memorable and an enjoyable experience.

– Charles F. Adams

Contents

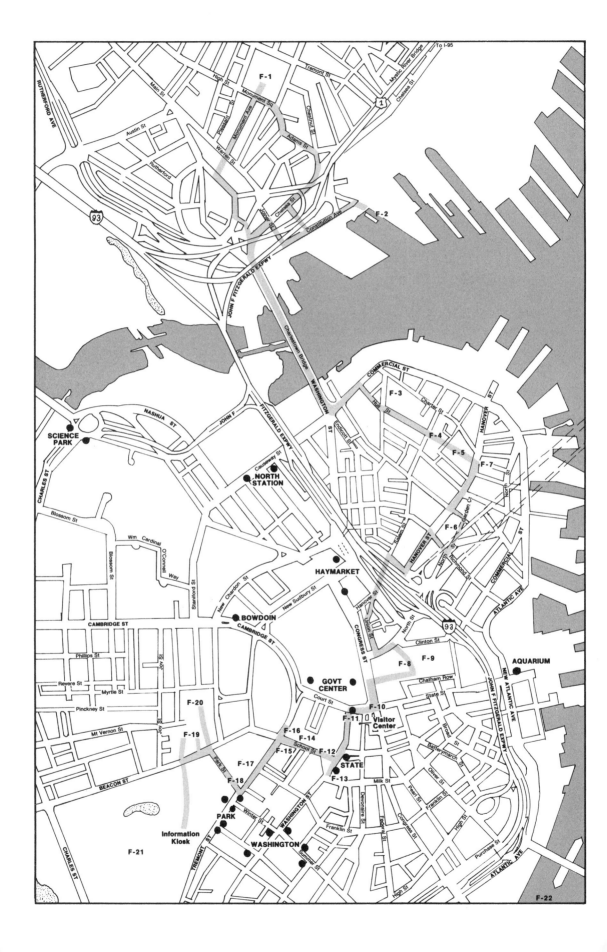

The **Freedom Trail** is a walking tour of Boston's major historic sites and structures. A red line marked on the sidewalk directs you from site to site. Begin your walking tour at any point, but if you desire to take the whole tour, plan an entire day for the three-mile round trip.

Information concerning Boston and the Freedom Trail can be obtained at the kiosk on Boston Common, at the Park visitor Center, and at the Charlestown Navy Yard.

About this map:

● Indicates Entrance/Exit for Rapid Transit stations. The name of the station is printed on the map near the ●

F Indicates the location of a Freedom Trail site or structure. The number following the F corresponds to the number on the list below.

☐ Grey line indicates Freedom Trail walking tour route.

Freedom Trail Sites & Structures
(the number responds to a location number on the map on the opposite page.)

1 Bunker Hill Monument
2 USS *Constitution*
3 Copp's Hill Burying Ground
4 Old North Church
5 Paul Revere Mall
6 Paul Revere's House
7 Saint Stephen's Church
8 Faneuil Hall
9 Quincy Market
10 Boston Massacre Marker
11 Old State House
12 Old Corner Bookstore
13 Old South Meeting House
14 Benjamin Franklin Statue
15 Site of the First Public School
16 King's Chapel and Burying Ground
17 Old Granary Burying Ground
18 Park Street Church
19 State House
20 The Beacon
21 Boston Common
22 The *Beaver*

Faneuil Hall
Dock Square

Faneuil Hall once dominated Boston's waterfront, "a handsome large brick building" that had presided over a welter of laborers, warehouses, and merchant vessels since 1742, when the eminent merchant Peter Faneuil presented the town with an elegant new two-story market building (downstairs) and town hall (upstairs) situated at the head of the seaport's Town Dock.

Dead within a year of the building's completion. Faneuil, the son of a French Huguenot refugee was eulogized as "the most public-spirited man, in all regards, that ever yet appeared on the northern continent of America." Mr. Faneuil's hall, inspired by the great mercantile structures of London and crowned with the famous green-eyed gilt grasshopper weathervane, has become a shrine of something that the doughty Peter Faneuil never dreamed — American independence.

For twenty years the structure served as the centerpiece of an orderly and prosperous colonial town, the affairs of which were conducted one flight up from a marketplace teeming with sellers and buyers of the countryside's produce. But a disastrous fire in 1761, which necessitated the virtual recon-

1

Faneuil Hall

struction of the Hall, seemed to herald a change in Boston. Here, in its heart, a new spirit was forged, as the colonial town began to articulate its desire for liberty.

In tumultuous town meetings and midnight assemblies Boston's orators thundered their opposition to the Navigation Acts and the Intolerable Acts, and all acts of the Crown which would restrict the traditional rights and privileges of New England. Here, the inheritors of a new world, the creators of a new order, finally claimed the rights of free men. James Otis, "a flame of fire," seared the Em-

pire with his eloquent insistence on the inalienable rights of the individual. Sam Adams, the foremost Son of Liberty, a ceaseless fomenter and a skillful demagogue, led the Boston town meeting to vote its adamant "opposition of Tyrants and their Minions." Oratory begot direct and even reckless action. One night in 1765 a well-liquored crowd, infuriated by enforcement of the Stamp Act, gathered at Faneuil Hall by the light of a bonfire and proceeded to attack the homes of Crown officials, literally tearing apart the Governor's mansion. Such were the passions which led to Revolution, nurtured here in Boston's Cradle of Liberty.

Post-Revolutionary growth and prosperity dictated the need for a larger town hall and market building, and so Faneuil Hall was greatly enlarged by the town's chief selectman and architect, Charles Bulfinch. Retaining and repeating the Doric and Tuscan pilasters and the arched windows of the painter John Smibert's 1742 design, Bulfinch doubled the size of the original 40'x100' structure, added a spacious third story of his own Ionic composition, and repositioned the grasshopper's cupola. The success of this 1805 undertaking is self-evident, and has required no further improvement.

In 1825 Boston filled in the old Town Dock area, and the town's demand for market space was satisfied by the construction of the Quincy Market buildings, which have recently been restored to their original purpose. Waterfront development and infill continued throughout the nineteenth century, eventually stranding Faneuil Hall in the middle of a modern city's downtown area; but Boston has never failed to honor Peter Faneuil's gift. In 1898 the Hall was thoroughly renovated and fireproofed, and today, as in the past, it serves as a handsome market and place of public meeting, presiding over a scene fully as busy and as colorful as in the days of merchant shipping and revolutionary zeal.

Quincy Market
Opposite Faneuil Hall

Boston became a city in 1822, and in 1823 Josiah Quincy was elected its Mayor for the first of five terms. The dynamic Quincy (1772-1864) greatly improved municipal services and pioneered in the areas of public health and safety, setting an example for cities everywhere. He soon turned his attention to the question of how to improve and enlarge Boston's limited market facilities "without great expense to the city"; and in the shabby stalls and stagnant waters near the Town Dock he found an answer.

Braving widespread doubt and criticism, Mayor Quincy ordered a landfill; and where wharf rats had scurried there arose a central marketplace. Designed by the progressive Boston architect Alexander Parris (1780-1852), the huge (50'x535') two-story market building, with its Greek porticoes and its domed central pavilion, was constructed in 1825 of granite from the quarries of Quincy, Massachusetts.

The sale of the newly-created land paid for the entire project; the flanking brick warehouses, and other structures built on the six new streets, added greatly to the tax base. Josiah Quincy, later President of Harvard, had created a vast and elegant market complex in one year, and in so doing had filled his city's coffers. Today, the Quincy Market-

place, newly redeveloped by
James Rowse, constitutes one of
the finest urban shopping
and dining areas in the world.

Quincy Market

Boston Massacre

Congress and State Streets

Boston had persistently and sometimes violently defied the authority of the Crown throughout the 1760s. Each new restrictive act had met with firm opposition and noncompliance, and by 1768 the royal officials feared an outright insurrection was at hand. In October, 1768, Boston was invaded and occupied by British troops; but their presence served only to spur the Sons of Liberty to greater resistance, and for two years the town smouldered. In the summer of 1769 the Royal Governor fled to England, bringing "effective regular government" to an end. By early 1770 Bostonians were openly clashing with the Redcoats, and armed conflict seemed inevitable.

On the evening of March 5, 1770, a band of townsmen provoked two soldiers into a fight, thrashed them, and then, fearing reprisal, sounded the alarm for general action. The bells pealed, and people poured into the streets, gathering in a large crowd at the Old State House, where they surrounded a lone British sentinel. British troops were dispatched to the scene, and the crowd became an abusive mob, waving clubs and threatening bloody murder, taunting the soldiers and calling out "Come on, you rascals, you bloody-backs, you lobster scoundrels – fire if you dare, God damn you, fire and be damned!"

The soldiers, pelted with snowballs and rocks, scorned and reviled, stood in fear for their lives; one of them, walloped by a stick, broke down and fired, and the rest followed suit, discharging their muskets pointblank at their tormentors. The mob scattered, carrying away the stricken; but three men lay dead, and two more would die of their wounds. Blood had been shed, lives had been lost, in the little circle in front of the State House. The Sons of Liberty had their martyrs, and Boston would never be the same.

The entire countryside erupted, and Minutemen prepared to march on Boston to drive the British into the sea. Wholesale slaughter was averted when the Redcoat regiments withdrew to a fort in the Harbor, and the soldiers who had fired that night were surrendered to stand trial. Though all but two were acquitted of manslaughter, the Boston Massacre ever afterwards served as a rallying point for the rebel cause, and was commemorated each March fifth with an oration lest Bostonians forget the night that "our streets were stained with the Blood of our Brethren, our ears were wounded by the groans of the dying, and our eyes were tormented with the sight of the mangled bodies of the Dead." Later, President John Adams would declare that "On that night the foundation of American independence was laid."

Artist's rendering
of the Boston Massacre

© Jack Frost

Old State House

206 Washington Street

From the first, this was the center of the town's public life: at the intersection of the two main roads (then known as King Street and the Road to the Neck; now State and Washington Streets) was a large open-air market plaza where all of Boston purchased its food and met to gossip. Nearby stood the first meeting-house (house of worship) as well as the homes of prominent citizens like Gov. John Winthrop and Capt. Robert Keayne, the latter a prosperous merchant tailor who, at his death in 1656, left funds for the construction of the first Town House. It was intended to shelter "the country people that come with their provisions" and to provide a meeting-place for merchants, an armory for the artillery company, a library for the learned, and chambers for the Great and General Court, the representative assembly of the colony of the Massachusetts Bay. Erected in the middle of the marketplace in 1657, the two-story structure served its purposes admirably until consumed in the great fire of 1711, the production of a "poor sottish woman" burning trash.

From the ashes of the old Town House rose a fine new brick building, two and a half stories high, surmounted by a cupola and adorned at its eastern end with the lion and the unicorn of the King. It was dedicated to the use of the General Court, the Royal Governor and his Council, and the various Courts of Justice. Here, at the head of the broad street leading up from newly-built Long Wharf, was conducted all the governmental business of the Province, and here the colonial cases were tried and decided.

Alarmed by a growing independence of spirit in Massachu-

Old State House

setts, the King had appointed a Royal Governor in 1692 to rule over his colony, but the representative assembly refused to be ruled. By the 1720s the General Court had come to resent the Governor's authority to the extent that it refused to pay his salary. The Governor, in turn, challenged the powers of the Court and suspended its privileges. Governors came and Governors went, and the representatives of the people of Massachusetts continued the struggle for power — which would end, a generation later, in outright rebellion.

Occasionally, the citizenry expressed itself directly, as in 1747 when a mob, incensed at the Royal Navy's impressment of Americans, marched on the Town House and shattered its windows, forcing Gov. Shirley to appear at the balcony and deliv-

Old State House, Western facade

er a conciliatory speech. And of course it was in Town House Square that the Boston Massacre took place. In 1748, through unknown agency, the Town House was again gutted by flames, soon to be rebuilt and restored to its former elegance. Throughout the 1760s liberty's spokesmen voiced their opposition to British policy in these halls: here Adams and Hancock inspired their peers, and here James Otis delivered his impassioned four-hour speech on the sanctity of individual rights, causing John Adams to declare that "Then and there, the child Independence was born."

The child grew up here, and by 1774 the General Court had become a rebel Congress, fleeing from British-held Boston and regrouping at Lexington, where war broke out in the spring of 1775. One year later, after the evacuation of the Redcoats from Boston, this building again became the seat of government — the independent government of the Commonwealth of Massachusetts. Rechristened, with a large American eagle adorning its western facade, the State House served as the setting of George Washington's triumphal 1789 return to Boston, a celebration nearly ruined by Gov. Hancock's initial snubbing of the new President.

After 1795 the State House building saw strange and varied service as a firehouse, a newspaper office, and, from 1830 to 1862, as Boston's City Hall. By 1881, city fathers were undecided about its utility; some, on learning that the commercial value of the site was $1,500,000, urged the demolition of the old building — whereupon the city of Chicago offered to purchase it for re-erection on the shores of Lake Michigan, a plan so inimical to Bostonians that the old State House was immediately given a complete restoration. Today, as the headquarters of the Bostonian Society and its excellent museum, the Old State House retains its dignity amidst the skyscrapers of the New Boston, a perpetual symbol of American freedom.

Franklin's Birthplace

17 Milk Street

In 1682 Josiah Franklin, an English dyer, came to Boston and married as his second wife Abiah Foulger of Nantucket, who was to increase his family to seventeen children. Franklin soon entered into the messy and malodorous business of soap-boiling, and, as a tallow-chandler (maker and seller of candles), had a modest wood-frame family residence built on Milk Street in 1691. Here, in 1706, the fifteenth child was born, christened with the name of Benjamin Franklin.

The boy attended Boston's Latin School, acquired a taste for books and a distaste for soap-boiling, and was appreticed to his older brother James, a printer. "In a little time," he later recorded, "I made great proficiency in the business, and became a useful hand to my brother." In addition to his duties as typesetter, pressman, and newsboy, young Ben wrote some topical verse which was published in broadside form; and soon he was contributing, anonymously, to his brother's newspaper, the New-England Courant.

The two quarrelled, however, and Benjamin bitterly resented his brother/master's abusive treatment. "His harsh and tyrannical treatment of me (was) a means of impressing me with that aversion to arbitrary power that has stuck to me thro' my whole life," he later wrote. Armed with a love of politics and of writing, the self-reliant seventeen-year-old Franklin secured a release from his indenture and booked passage for Philadelphia, leaving Boston behind as he embarked on the great adventure that his life would become.

Artist's rendering of Franklin's Birthplace

Old South Meeting House
Washington Street

The Old South Meeting House stands on the site of the original meeting-house built in 1669 as a place of worship for the South End congregation, newly gathered as Boston's Third Religious Society. It was a typical Puritan structure, severe in its lines and devoid of a steeple or anything else that might give it the appearance of a church. To the Puritans a church was a building in which the rites of the Church of England were observed, and they had broken from that church and its Popish liturgy. In their eyes, a plain barnlike meeting-house was as acceptable to God as any cathedral in Christendom.

Two generations of prosperity and theological evolution made it possible for the by-then fashionable South End congregation to build a new house of worship in the latest "Georgian" style; and so in 1729 the Third Religious Society pulled down the old building and in its place raised the brick structure now known as the Old South Meeting House. Designed by Robert Twelves and built by Josiah Blanchard, the massive building featured a tower, belfry, and steeple that gave it the unmistakable appearance of a church; but of course to the congregation it was still a meeting-house.

In the 1760s the Old South was frequently used for mass gatherings and town meetings too large to fit into Faneuil Hall. One such rally – the largest ever – occurred on the afternoon of December 16, 1773. Thousands of people crowded the meeting-house and thronged the streets outside as Sam Adams orated on the non-importation of certain British goods, particularly those to be found in the holds of three recently-arrived merchant vessels. After Adams came Josiah Quincy, who sensed in the meeting's outrage and the Governor's intransigence the makings of a mighty tempest. "I see the clouds which now rise thick and fast upon the horizon," he declaimed. "The thunders roll and the lightnings play, and to the God who rides on the whirlwind and directs the storm I commit my country!" At that, the crowd let out a mighty whoop, and off it surged, torches blazing, down to the waterfront for an evening Tea Party.

Right up to the outbreak of war, the Old South

Old South Meeting House

Old South Meeting House

Meeting House served as a rebel auditorium as well as a place of worship. Perhaps no structure in Boston was so readily identified with the patriotic cause; and for that reason the British took special revenge when the opportunity presented itself. During the years that the Redcoats occupied Boston (June, 1774 to June, 1776) the Old South was used as an officer's club and a riding academy, with a liquor dispensary in the gallery. The pulpit was torn down, and the high box floor pews were broken up for kindling. In the large open area thus created, several tons of dirt were dumped and raked smooth; and here, where the word of God and of man had rung out, the Queen's Light Dragoons spurred their mounts round and round, sometimes to drunken applause from the gallery above.

After the British had been expelled from Boston, the congregation returned to its meetinghouse and rebuilt the interior as it was before; the people of the town continued to hold overflow meetings here. The only lasting effect of the British presence was the loss of many valuable documents, including the manuscript of the Pilgrim Governor Bradford's History of Plymouth. It was only by accident that these priceless papers were discovered in England some fifty years later.

Twice the Old South has nearly gone up in smoke. In December, 1810 the roof caught fire and the building seemed doomed; but a courageous mastmaker named Isaac Harris proved to be more than a match for the flames. In gratitude for his superhuman rooftop exertions, the Third Religious Society presented him with an elegant silver water pitcher, now on display at the Museum of Fine Arts. Unfortunately, Isaac Harris was unavailable in 1872, when the greatest of all Great Boston Fires destroyed 65 acres of the downtown area; and yet his spirit must have been present, for the conflagration was halted just short of the Old South by the judicious dynamiting of nearby structures.

Having been preserved from the ravages of fire, the Old South Meeting House soon faced obliteration in the name of progress. After bitter debate, the congregation had built a New Old South in the Back Bay in 1875, and put its former home up for sale. Located on an extremely valuable commercial site, the noble old building seemed doomed to the wrecker's ball; however, in a remarkable burst of civic pride, Boston rallied. An Old South Association was formed, and in short order raised the $400,000 purchase price – the first instance of urban historic preservation in America. The Association continues to maintain the Old South today, operating it as neither a church nor a meetinghouse, but as a memorial to the days and the deeds of Adams, Quincy, and all the others who helped create a new nation.

The Old Corner Bookstore

Washington and School Streets

In 1712, the year after one of Boston's many Great Fires had reduced the neighborhood to cinders, Thomas Crease had this solid brick house built as his residence and apothecary shop. With its steep gambrel roof, brick belt courses, and corner quoins, it was one of the handsomest houses in a town of about ten thousand souls, almost all of whom had recourse to the herbs and potions of druggist Crease. It is doubtful that the new owner, with his progressive English-style townhouse and his flourishing business, had any idea that this land was once the property of William Hutchinson and his wife Anne. She was a brilliant woman whose compelling religious teachings led to a dangerous Puritan schism in 1630s Boston, resolved only by her banishment from the colony. It is fitting that this site has such strong intellectual and commercial associations, for a publishing house draws on both, and it is as a publishing house and bookstore that the building is chiefly known.

By the 1820s the area had become commercial and the Crease house was being used as a bookshop by a young publisher named William Ticknor. The firm of Ticknor and Reed, thanks to scrupulous honesty and the then-novel practice of paying royalties, secured the rights to publish American editions of the leading English authors; and a new partner, the engaging James Fields, soon enabled the company to sign contracts with the New England authors who were then virtually creating an American literature. By midcentury Ticknor and Fields Inc. was publishing the works of Henry Wadsworth Longfellow, Harriet Beecher Stowe, Nathaniel Hawthorne, Ralph Waldo Emerson, John Greenleaf Whittier, Oliver Wendell Holmes, and Henry D. Thoreau; moreover, the office/bookstore had become the city's literary center, an informal clubhouse where a writer could always find good conversation and an extra glass of claret. Out of these encounters grew the famous Saturday Club, whose members were the backbone of the house magazine, the Atlantic Monthly.

Eventually the Old Corner Bookstore outgrew its original building and moved to larger quarters, after which the old Crease house began a very gradual decline, ending as an unrecognizable billboard-covered pizza joint. In 1960, with encouragement from the city, a benevolent group purchased the building and promptly restored it to its original appearance. Since

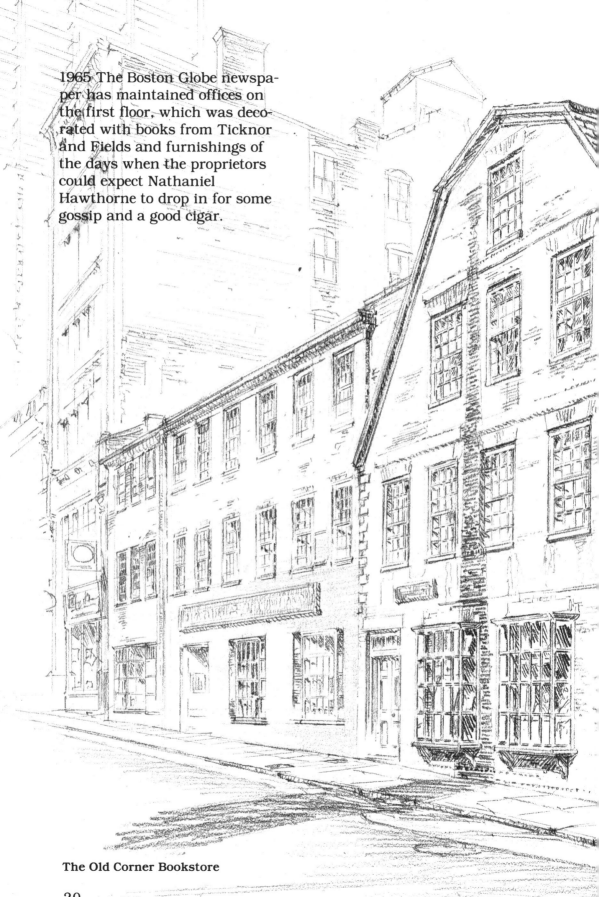

1965 The Boston Globe newspaper has maintained offices on the first floor, which was decorated with books from Ticknor and Fields and furnishings of the days when the proprietors could expect Nathaniel Hawthorne to drop in for some gossip and a good cigar.

The Old Corner Bookstore

20

Ben Franklin's Statue
Old City Hall grounds

Here stands Silence Dogood and Poor Richard; a printer, stove-contriver, kite-flyer, and declaration-signer – the remarkable Benjamin Franklin, in bronze, back in his hometown of Boston. Given Franklin's long association with France, it is not inappropriate that he stands in front of the Old City Hall, which was built in 1862 in the fashionable French Second Empire style (on the site of Bulfinch's 1810 Court House); and though he never met Major Josiah Quincy, with whom he shares this outlook, both men were Latin School scholars, and each would have found an admirer in the other.

Benjamin Franklin (1706-90) was the greatest American of his day, an inventor, editor, military officer, politician, and statesman whose public career began in Boston at the age of thirteen, when, under the pseudonym of Mrs. Silence Dogood, he contributed essays and articles to his brother's newspaper. Leaving Boston for Philadelphia at seventeen, he soon voyaged to London, published there his "Dissertation on Liberty and Necessity, Pleasure and Pain," and was back in Philadelphia by 1726, writing tracts and publishing his own newspaper. In 1732 be began the witty and worldly "Poor Richard's Almanac," which helped to define the newly emerging American character.

Elected to public office, he formed a fire company and a police force, and in his spare time invented the Franklin stove. In the 1740s he established the University of Pennsylvania and the American Philosophical Society, and became a military officer; in the 1750s he flew a kite in a storm, proposed a plan for the union of the colonies, served as a Colonel in the French & Indian War, paved Philadelphia's streets, published the "Way to Wealth," and departed for England as Pennsylvania's agent there. Throughout the 1760s and 1770s he acted in behalf of the cause of independence both here and in Europe, and during the War it was he who engineered the treaty of alliance with France. A signer of the Declaration, a framer of the Constitution, America's first and greatest genius, Franklin's formal education consisted of a few years at the Latin School in Boston, a city that, having formed his char-

acter for the benefit of Philadelphia, America, and the world, is proud to claim him as a native son.

Before moving on, observe that the sculptor, Richard Greenough, in contemplating the countenance of his subject, "found the left side of the great man's face philosophical and reflective, and the right side funny and smiling." And so he remains.

BENJAMIN FRANKLIN
BORN IN BOSTON, 17 JANUARY 1706.
DIED IN PHILADELPHIA 17 APRIL, 1790

Franklin's Print Shop

Josiah Franklin, the father of seventeen children, had determined that each of his ten sons should have a different trade. One, James, was packed off to London to learn "the art or mystery" of a printer, a rare calling in New England. Returning to Boston in 1719, he soon established a printing shop, and in 1721 launched a newspaper, the New-England Courant, which soon put the existing Boston News-Letter out of business. Josiah's youngest son, Benjamin, originally intended for the ministry, was apprenticed to his brother, and "Silence Dogood's" sprightly contributions helped ensure the new paper's success.

James Franklin was a good printer and an excellent newspaperman, with a sure sense of what his readers wanted to know. This ability to reflect his townsmen's real interests and opinions inevitably gave offense to the conservative Massachusetts General Court, which imprisoned him for a month, during which time young Ben ran the paper and continued "to give our rulers some rubs in it." James was finally released with the injunction that he was not to print the Courant; and so it was published under the name of brother Benjamin.

Setting type by hand, absorbing the literary and political influences of the newspaper office/pressroom, printing books, broadsides, and circulars and hawking them on the street, Benjamin Franklin obtained the best informal education a hard-working printer's devil could hope for, and turned it to excellent advantage – in Philadelphia.

Artist's rendering of what Franklin's print shop may have looked like.

Site of the
First Public School
School Street

On School Street stood the first public school in America, known as Boston Latin School, founded in 1636 to prepare scholars for the newly established Harvard College in Cambridge. The first schoolmaster was Mr. Philemon Pormont, who relinquished his duties to Daniel Maude in 1638. Here such noted early Bostonians as Cotton Mather, Benjamin Franklin, John Hancock and Samuel Adams received a classical education, the beginnings of a tradition that continues to this day. The Boston Public Latin School, situated elsewhere in the city, still produces superior scholars, many of whom pursue their higher education at the College in Cambridge.

Old Granary
Tremont Street

Boston is proud of its old graveyards with their illustrious dead and their quaint inscriptions and their sense of repose. The Old Granary Burying Ground combines all of these elements in a way that is almost irresistible, luring the passerby from the traffic and noise of Tremont Street into this fascinating sanctuary of the past. Here are buried three signers of the Declaration of Independence (John Han-

**Old Granary
Burying Ground**

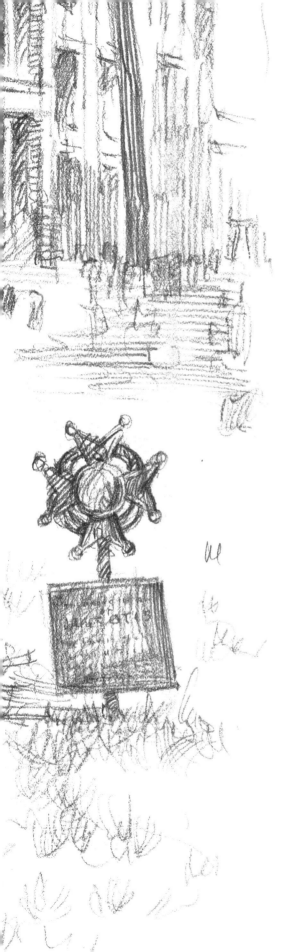

cock, Samuel Adams, Robert Treat Paine), eight governors, the five victims of the Boston Massacre, scores of Revolutionary soldiers, Paul Revere, Peter Faneuil, the diarist Samuel Sewall, the city's first mayor, John Phillips, Benjamin Franklin's parents, and the ordinary men, women and children who comprised the little world of early Boston.

In 1660 a part of the town Common was appropriated for use as a South End cemetery, known as the South Burying Ground. Many of the seventeenth-century stones still stand, richly lettered and carved with ghastly death's heads and emblems of the fruits of paradise, Puritan symbols of the departing soul and the blissful eternity that is its destination. Among these markers is the 1690 stone of Mary Goose, who, although a mother, was not Mother Goose. That literary personage was Elizabeth, who, as the second wife of Isaac Goose, had charge of so many children (twenty) that it is perfectly possible that indeed she did not know what to do.

In 1737 the town granary, a large building used to store reserves of wheat and other grains for distribution to the poor, was erected between the graveyard (where pigs were allowed to browse) and the rest of the Common (where cows were turned

Old Granary Burying Ground

29

**Old Granary
Burying Ground**

30

31

out to graze). In 1738, one door up, the town built its Workhouse, where the indigent and unfortunate were forced to earn an income. And so here was a rather stark moral streetscape: repositories of the staff of life, of failed hopes and hard labor, and of triumphant death – a Puritan triptych.

On the site of the Granary and the Workhouse stands the beautiful Park Street Church, built in 1809, a welcome change from its gloomy predecessor and something of a counterpoint to the heavily symbolic granite front of the Old Granary Burying Ground, with its winged globe and its downturned torches and its flying dumbbells, hourglasses whose time has run out.

Originally, the various families buried their dead in separate plots, but some later sexton rearranged the headstones in rows,

the better to mow the grass with his scythe. In addition to its famous dead, the Old Granary harbors some very interesting characters, among them Ann Pollard, who, as a child, was the first of the settlers to hop ashore at Shawmut (later known as Boston). She grew up and gave birth to a numerous progeny and followed an independent pipe-smoking course, operating the wild and woolly Horse Shoe Tavern for many decades and having her portrait painted at the age of a hundred and three (it still hangs at Old South Meeting House). Two years later she died and was buried here, survived by 113 descendants and mourned by the whole town.

Young Benjamin Woodbridge found his way into this resting place as a result of an injudicious remark made at the Royal Exchange – the merchants' gathering-place – in the summer of 1728. He was challenged to a duel with swords, accepted, and the affair of honor, held on Boston Common, ended with his being run through with a rapier at the age of twenty. More happy is the story of Elisha Brown, who, during the British occupation of Boston, single-handedly prevented an entire regiment of His Majesty's troops from dispossessing him of his spacious home, which they coveted as a barracks, and in which he died a peaceful death many years later. His story, etched in stone, is one of the thousands of Boston stories interred in the Old Granary.

Park Street Church

*Corner of Tremont and
Park Streets*

Park Street Church, built in
1809, stands on the site of the
town's Old Granary, a huge barn
that became so infested with
rats and weevils that the town
had to sell it, whereupon the
new owners cleaned out both
grain and vermin, and reused it
for commercial purposes (including a sail-loft where Old Ironsides' first suit of sails was
stitched). The Granary was
finally torn down, and its timbers used to build a tavern elsewhere in town.

Soon after the razing of the
Old Granary building, a new and

Park Street Church

very different structure rose in its place: the elegant brick edifice of the Park Street Church, a trinitarian evangelical religious society that was deeply committed to the orthodox Puritan form of worship, and looked with horror upon the rising tide of Unitarianism. Given this conservative attitude, it may be significant that the congregation chose for its architect not the popular designers of Federal Boston, Charles Bulfinch or Asher Benjamin, but Peter Banner, an Englishman who had recently come to Boston from Connecticut, where he had designed buildings for Yale University. Whatever the inspiration, it was a wise choice, for Banner designed a masterpiece of ecclesiastical architecture, considered by the august Boston novelist Henry James to be "perfectly felicitous" in its appearance, "the most interesting mass of brick and mortar in America."

Park Street Church presents an extremely graceful facade with its bowfront colonnades, Palladian tower window, recessed arches, carved wooden detail (by Boston's Solomon Willard), pedimented belfry, and towering steeple – once even taller, but diminished in the nineteenth century after a bad spell of swaying. Banner drew on nearly every element of Bulfinch's residential design vocabulary, infused it with the grace of the London spires of Sir Christopher Wren, and produced a monument so striking and so enduring that the congregation has remained here ever since, although not without occasional sacrifices.

Despite its superior commercial site, Park Street Church has never been endangered by sale and possible demolition; however, there was a difficult time when it was necessary to rent out part of the building as a tea room, until it was found that women were displeasing the Lord by smoking cigarettes there. Perhaps the greatest concession to its downtown location came on a Sunday morning in November, 1895, as the reverend pastor sat in his study working on a sermon. Suddenly the windows came crashing in, and the man of God found himself fighting for survival in an avalanche of mud. He escaped with his life, but the study was ruined and his evening sermon, so lovingly prepared, had disappeared. It was then discovered that a

Park Street Church

workman, digging the tunnel for the world's first sub-way system, on a Sunday morning in the very shadow of the church, had broken a huge water main. That evening the minister delivered a sermon filled with righteous Puritan wrath, denouncing the subway as "an infernal hole" and suggesting that none other than Satan himself had been responsible for this "unchristian outrage." He was probably right.

This church is associated with other "firsts." Here, on the Fourth of July, 1829, the great abolitionist and publisher of the Liberator, Newburyport's William Lloyd Garrison, gave his first public antislavery address — an oration which was not well-received by his auditors, who at one point tried to lynch him. On Independence Day three years later, the song "America" was first sung; and here, in 1849, Senator Charles Sumner delivered his powerful oration, "The War System of Nations," to the American Peace Society.

The corner of the Common opposite the church has long been known as "Brimstone Corner," in part because a load of brimstone was stored in the cellar of the church during the War of 1812, and in part as a tribute to the many hellfire-and-brimstone sermons thundered out from the Park Street pulpit. This corner has also seen its share of momentous modern events, such as the world's largest crap-game, held here during the Boston police strike of 1919 and violently dispersed by the bayonet-wielding state militia. More recently, Brimstone Corner has played host to Vietnam War protesters, mimes, saffron-robed Buddhists, street actors and musicians, fruit vendors, and newsstands, a colorful and shifting scene dominated by the splendor of Peter Banner's masterpiece.

Boston Common

*Bounded by Park, Tremont, Boylston
and Charles Streets*

Boston Common is the oldest public park in America.
When John Winthrop and his Puritan followers first
pitched their tents on the peninsula of Shawmut, they
found a learned hermit, Reverend William Blackstone,
on the slope of Beacon Hill, overlooking a pleasant expanse of meadow which ran down to the "Back Bay"
on its western side. Rev. Mr. Blackstone was allowed to
keep fifty acres of this land as his homestead; but the
solitary bachelor was not inclined to share so much
company. In 1634 for 30£ he sold his homestead to the
town (withholding six acres at the top of the hill) and
vanished into the countryside. He next appeared in
Boston a few years later, riding a bull and looking for
a wife.

Boston realized the value of open space, and in 1640
it was "ordered, that no more land be granted in the
town out of the open ground or common field, which is
between Sentry Hill and Mr. Colbron's end." And so
the Common was reserved for such important public
uses as pasturage for goats and cows, a military
parade ground for the local "train-band" or militia,
and, of course, a place of execution.

It was not difficult to commit a capital offense in
early Boston, which took the Old Testament quite literally; and nothing was quite as crowd-pleasing as the
hanging of a witch or the member of a prohibited religious sect. Here William Robinson and Marmaduke
Stevenson, convicted Quakers, were launched into
eternity; and here Mary Dyer, Margaret Jones, and
Mistress Anne Hibbins, proven consorts of His Satanic
Majesty, were expunged from the Divine State. Here
too, for unspecified crimes against the settlers, Matoo-
nas, an Indian sagamore, was tied to a tree and shot
in 1656. Each of these events attracted great crowds of
onlookers and was cause for a general holiday.

More prosaically, in the days before sanitary land-
fills the Common served as an admirable town dump.
It was soon found necessary to pass a law commanding that "no person shall throw forth or lay any en-
trails of beasts or fowls, or garbage, or carrion, or dead
dogs or cats, or any other dead beast or stinking thing,

in any way, on the Common, but are enjoined to bury all such things so they may prevent all annoyance unto any." The burial of deceased Puritans also became a matter of some concern, and in 1660 a part of the Common was set aside as a graveyard, now known as the Old Granary Burying Ground.

The Common had three ponds for the town's thirsty cattle: the Frog Pond, now institutionalized as a bathing-place for children and other waders and splashers; the stagnant old Horse Pond, connected by a ditch to the low marsh of the riverbank, and long since filled up; and another pond, now gone, which remained nameless until the early 1800s, when the rapist Mr. Sheehan was executed on its banks.

Trees are conspicuous adornments of the present Common, as they must have been in 1630; but soon enough almost all had been cut down for firewood. By 1722 only three trees stood here, two near Brimstone Corner (across from Park Street Church) and another, the Old Elm, stood in the middle of the Common well into the nineteenth century. The Old Elm, also known as the Great Elm and the Great Tree, was standing when Winthrop arrived, and from its branches colonial malefactors were hanged. Under its noble bulk young Ben Woodbridge was killed in the only duel known to have taken place here. The venerable old great elm tree was

still (barely) standing in 1872, the object of profound civic reverence. The tree situation had improved soon after 1722, and by 1735 a double colonnade of trees paralleled Tremont Street and provided the town's most fashionable promenade, The Mall.

In keeping with the resolve of 1640, very few structures have ever been built on the Common. An Almshouse, which housed the poor, aged, and infirm (no beggars in Boston!); was built in 1662, but burned down in 1682. Its replacement served as an abode for criminals as well as charity cases, an unfortunate situation which was "corrected" before 1722 with the construction of a Park Street Bridewell or House of Correction, which the criminals shared with the insane. A huge old granary was built in 1737 next to the South Burying Ground; from it, corn and wheat were distributed in times of need. The Workhouse, built next to the granary in 1738, was the temporary home of "rogues and vagabonds" and other carefree types. There was also the Old Powder House, built in 1706 out near the Frog Pond and used to store the town's munitions.

In the days shortly before the Revolution the Common was a sorry sight, covered with tents and mess buildings and latrines, and swarming with foreign sol-

Boston Common

40

41

diers wearing red coats. Where once the Ancient and Honorable Artillery Company had drilled in sometimes tipsy disarray, the British troops of occupation now wheeled in precise formation, grimly training for the day of revenge against their Yankee tormentors. As it happened, the Redcoats were severely beaten in both Boston-area battles. When George Washington's new army, perched atop Dorchester Heights, compelled His Majesty's troops to evacuate old Boston, they indulged their feelings of vengeance by chopping down the trees along The Mall.

After independence was won and Boston had begun to prosper under the new Republic, the Common was recognized as one of the chief assets of the town. Charles Bulfinch was given free rein to transform its surroundings. Beginning in 1791 with the home of Dr. John Joy, Bulfinch designed elegant townhouses for the crest of Beacon Hill, a development that soon became the town's most fashionable address.

He later turned his attention to Park Street. By 1803 all of the public buildings – Workhouse, Almshouse, Bridewell, Granary, etc. – had been razed, and in their stead rose magnificent four-story common-wall residences known as Park Row. After the triumph of Park Row (vestiges of which still stand),

Bulfinch engineered the sale of town land along Tremont Street, opposite The Mall. This sale paid for the erection of a new Almshouse far away from the Common, and enabled the great Bulfinch to design a magnificent series of buildings in the style of Park Row. Built on Tremont Street facing the sacred Mall, these residences were unified by a wonderful eighty-pillar Doric colonnade. By 1815, then, Charles Bulfinch had framed Boston Common with three solid walls of the finest architecture in America.

Boston Common today presents the beholder with a delightful expanse of trees and grass and statuary, unsurpassed by any other urban park in the country. It encompasses baseball diamonds, graveyards, underground parking garages, bandstands, flowerbeds, and cow paths. Here Emerson tried to persuade Walt Whitman to clean up his *Leaves of Grass,* and here Oliver Wendell Holmes discovered that the State House was "the hub of the solar system."

Soldiers and Sailors Monument in Boston Common

State House
Beacon and Park Streets

Charles Bulfinch (1763-1844) was Boston's leading citizen for 25 years: as chief selectman, urban planner, superintendent of police, and pre-eminent architect, he transformed Boston from a haphazard collection of colonial buildings to a unified composition in Adamesque brick elegance, unmatched on the continent of North America. The State House, begun in 1795 and finished in 1798, is generally considered to be his crowning achievement.

Bulfinch was born into a wealthy and venerable upper-class Boston family, the son of a Harvard-educated physician who did not want his son to practice medicine. Upon graduation from Harvard in 1781, Charles went to work in the counting house of a family friend; but business was slow, and he usually was "at leisure to cultivate a taste for Architecture." He exercised his gifts in the design and improvement of several Boston residences, and so acquired an excellent reputation as a "gentleman designer." In the years 1785 to 1787 he made a grand tour of Europe. There, in the architecture of classical Rome and in the contemporary neoclassical designs of London, Bulfinch found a style that expressed the aspirations of the young American Republic.

Returning to Boston, he again enjoyed a "season of leisure, pursuing no business but giving gratuitous advice in architecture" to a growing list of clients, among whom was a committee of the Massachusetts General Court. Responding to their request for "a plan for a new state-house" – something grand and capacious, a fitting capitol for the new Commonwealth – Bulfinch submitted his design in November, 1787, explaining that it was "in the style of a building celebrated all over Europe," London's Somerset House, a monumental neo-Palladian government building on the Thames. More than seven years elapsed before the design was implemented. On July 4, 1795, amidst pomp and circumstance, the cornerstone was laid.

Originally intended for a site on the lower part of the Common, the new State House was built atop Beacon Hill only after Bulfinch had begun to design and build handsome private residences alongside the Hancock mansion, in the shadow of his eagle-topped Memorial Column. Progress was slow, and expenses were high. For two and a half years the masons, carpenters, plasterers, carvers, painters, glaziers and roofers labored to bring forth the colossus on the hill. In January, 1798 their work was done: under Bulfinch's supervision, they had built the finest public building in America.

The original redbrick Bulfinch facade generally resembles the pavilion of London's Somerset House, but in detail it is an original neoclassical Bulfinch composition, with blind-arched windows and elegant lunettes. The original building – including flanking brick pavilions – is 173 feet across the front, of which 94 feet is occupied by the arched brick portico which supports a magnificent Corinthian colonnade, in turn surmounted by a pilastered pediment. Above all rises the famous golden dome, 50 feet in diameter and 30 feet high, "a grand, dominating hemisphere" crowned by a pine-cone-topped cupola. The dome was originally painted a lead grey, but was sheathed in copper by Paul Revere and Sons in 1802. In 1861 it was gilded, and in 1874 gold-leafed. Except for a period during World War II when it was blacked out, the dome has gleamed in the sunlight for more than a century, the noblest sight in Boston.

The State House was an immediate success, acclaimed as "the most magnificent building in the Union," a marvel of "perfect taste and proportion." Its entry hall was no less handsome than the facade; and the lofty ceilings, ornamental plaster work (by Daniel Raynard), and richly carved columns and pilasters of the principal rooms were universally admired. Although the State House has been greatly enlarged over the years, and the interior extensively remodeled, the Bulfinch Front remains intact, an authentic American temple.

By a twist of fate, the private fortune of Charles Bulfinch was

State House

sinking just as his public reputation was reaching its height. Committing nearly all of his wealth to an ambitious residen-

tial development known as the Tontine Crescent in Franklin Street, Bulfinch was unable to weather one of the many financial panics of the early Republic. Unwilling to see its great citizen reduced to poverty, Boston in 1799 elected him the chief select-

man and superintendent of police. As the town's leading administrator/architect, he improved nearly every aspect of his native place, from the execution of laws and the conduct of government to the planning and laying out of new streets and the design of dozens of residential, commercial, ecclesiastical and institutional buildings. After two decades of service, Bulfinch was summoned to Washington, DC to become the architect of the

nation's capital. There he lived and worked for thirteen happy years. Returning to Boston in 1830, he spent his last years at the old Bulfinch mansion in Bowdoin Square, surrounded by his large family and honored by a grateful Boston.

From a lifetime of extraordinary accomplishment, it is difficult to claim pre-eminence for any one project; and yet the State House was Bulfinch's masterpiece. In one magnificent stroke he had introduced a new architecture for the new nation, powerful and majestic, expressive of the ideals embodied in the Constitution of a self-governing people. In Boston, America's first professional architect had set a new standard and applied it to every aspect of the town – a legacy of excellence that endures to this day.

State House

49

Artist's rendering of John Hancock's House

John Hancock's House

The house of John Hancock, by a series of regrettable circumstances, was torn down in 1863 – one of the last of the great Georgian mansions in Boston, as notable architecturally as it was historically. Built in 1737 for John's uncle Thomas Hancock, a wealthy merchant who had begun as a bookbinder and stationer, the house was composed of Connecticut stone, two stories high, with a gambrel roof, corner quoins, four large chimneys, an elegant rooftop captain's walk, and a richly-panelled interior – all in all, the house of an English squire. Situated in solitary splendor on the side of old Beacon Hill, overlooking the green expanse of the Common from a splendid setting of formal gardens and fruit trees, the estate passed on the death of Thomas in 1764 to his favorite nephew John, a high-living young merchant who was just beginning to espouse the cause of liberty.

Having inherited a fortune – helpful to someone who himself was not particularly adept at commerce – John Hancock plunged into the Revolutionary politics of the day, serving as moderator of the Boston town meeting, sitting as a member of the town's various rebel committees, and, later, becoming President of both the Massachusetts Revolutionary Congress and the Continental Congress as gathered in Philadelphia. His house was occupied by British soldiers at the time of the signing of the Declaration of Independence, which may well account for the boldness of his famous signature. A dandy with a talent for spending more money than he earned, Hancock served as first Governor of Massachusetts, and at the end of his life attempted to donate his house to the Commonwealth as a perpetual Governor's Mansion. The Commonwealth declined; his heirs persisted; and ignorance won out. The Hancock House was demolished in the midst of the Civil War.

The Beacon
Behind the State House

The highest of Boston's three hills, old Sentry Hill was used as a lookout from the beginning, and before long a beacon was erected there, to be lit in times of danger – thus the new name, Beacon Hill. During the years of rebellion the beacon was frequently set ablaze, and so when the structure blew down in 1789 it seemed an appropriate site for a monument "to commemorate the train of events which led to the American Revolution . . . ." Charles Bulfinch designed the original memorial column, sixty feet high, of stuccoed brick and stone and topped with an eagle weather-vane. In 1791 the column was erected to the applause of the city, and for twenty years it stood guard. In 1811 Beacon

Hill's crest was removed for landfill, and down came the column, to be rebuilt in its present location in 1865, still surmounted by Bulfinch's vigilant eagle.

The Beacon

King's Chapel
58 Tremont Street

Massive old King's chapel was completed in 1754 for an Anglican congregation on the site of the original chapel. In 1688, the detested Royal Governor Andros had appropriated a corner of the Puritan town's first graveyard, and built thereon a small wooden chapel, complete with spire, as Boston's first Episcopal house of worship. Though Andros was soon forced to flee, King's Chapel remained and grew, and in 1710 the building was enlarged. Here the Royal officials worshipped in handsome style, surrounded by opulent decoration and using a silver service donated by Dukes and Earls and even the King himself.

In 1741 Boston's Anglicans decided to replace the old wooden chapel with a London-style stone edifice; but the project was deferred until 1748, when funds were raised to retain the talents of Peter Harrison, a gentleman designer from Newport, Rhode Island. Harrison's final design called for a substantial stone building and tower, to be lightened by the "beautiful effect" of a lofty wooden steeple. His double row of windows, the lower smaller than the upper, caused one wit to comment that he "had heard of the Canons of the Church, but had never before seen the port-holes."

King's Chapel

The Wheelbarrow Walk beside King's Chapel

The granite came from Quincy (then called Braintree), which then had neither quarries nor mastery of the stone-dresser's art, thus accounting for the rough texture of the blocks. With much ceremony, the cornerstone was laid in August, 1749, and soon the great walls were rising around the old Chapel, which continued to be used as a sanctum sanctorum until 1753, when it was finally demolished and thrown out the windows of its successor. Unfortunately, for financial reasons the "beautiful effect" of Peter Harrison's steeple was never realized; nevertheless, the interior of the new church was a marvel of Georgian elegance – including the town's first organ – and the Anglicans were well pleased.

During the siege of Boston, the British military and naval officers worshipped here. After their hasty departure, Boston removed the King from the Chapel and rechristened it Stone Chapel, a name that didn't last. In 1790, shortly after George Washington attended an oratorio here, the colonnaded portico was added to the front. The final change took place about 1800, when the first Episcopal church in New England became the First Unitarian Church in America, whose congregation, summoned by Paul Revere's bell, continues to worship where once the King's officials said their prayers.

King's Chapel Burying Ground
Tremont Street

In 1630 Sir Isaac Johnson, a leader of the Massachusetts Bay Company, succumbed to the rigors of New England and was buried in the southwest corner of his garden lot; and as other Puritans followed him into paradise, their mortal husks were here interred. For thirty years this was the town's only burying ground, the last resting place of nearly the entire first generation of English settlers, including the worshipful Governor Winthrop, the pastors of the First Church, and other early notables. Here too – after the Episcopal Church was set down on one corner – were buried Governor William Shirley and other royal officials, as well as British soldiers. The present arrangement of the headstones is the work of an old-time Superintendent of Burials who apparently considered the beautifully carved old slates to be elements of a composition (his) rather than accurate grave markers. Perhaps for this reason, the old First Graveyard – or King's Chapel Burying Ground – is replete with legends of ghostly doings and postmortem restlessness.

King's Chapel Burying Ground

Paul Revere's House

Paul Revere's House

19 North Square

The North End's Paul Revere House is the only seventeenth-century wooden dwelling still standing in any major American city. Originally, this was the site of the house of the famous Increase Mather, autocratic minister of the Old North Church and father of his eminent successor, the diarist and witch-hunter, Rev. Cotton Mather.

The Great Fire of November 27, 1676 destroyed much of the North End, the Mather house included, and on its site a new house was built for a mariner, John Jeffs, who sold it to a merchant, Robert Howard, in 1681. This "new house" was built in the English style of the period, with a steep pitch roof, a front overhang and a gable overhang at attic level, both with pendant drops, and all contributing to an almost medieval effect. It was an unusually commodious house, with two large rooms in the front and two more in an original rear ell that extended back towards the garden. The whole structure was framed in heavy carved timbers held together by ingenious joinery and wooden pegs. Light was admitted through several diamond-paned casement windows, and heat (but not much) was provided by the large open fireplaces of the huge end-placed chimney.

Here Robert Howard and his successors dwelt one block from the sea, overlooking triangular North Square with its market, guard house, meeting-house and pump – a real beehive of industry and information, and one of the town's most fashionable neighborhoods. It was still a prime spot in 1770, when a goldsmith purchased the Howard house for 213£, 6/8, and moved in with his large family. The new owner, who took out a mortgage of 160£, was named Paul Revere.

Revere, the son of a French emigre named Anthoine Revoire, was the talented possessor of a wide variety of skills – and industry enough to make good use of them all. The proprietor of a Hancock's Wharf shop in which he fashioned objects of gold and silver, he was, as well, a copper-plate designer/engraver, a false-tooth manufacturer, the owner of a bell-foundry and copper works, the designer, engraver, and printer of the Commonwealth's paper money, a Son of Liberty and prominent rebel organizer, an excellent horseman who rode as official courier of the revolutionary congress, and the proud father of sixteen children. He also turned his hand to architecture and added a third story to the old house. In the age before specialization, he was Boston's pre-eminent generalist.

Revere today is remembered for his Midnight Ride rather than his bills and bells and bowls; and for that he has Henry

Paul Revere's House

©Jack Frost

Wadsworth Longfellow to thank. Published in 1863, Longfellow's ballad of "Paul Revere's Ride," with its galloping rhythms and stirring language, had made Paul the best-known hero of the American Revolution. With the possible exception of "The Night Before Christmas," "Paul Revere's Ride" may be the only poem of which every American can recite at least one couplet.

After his Revolutionary service, Revere settled down to life of hard and rewarding work as one of the nation's first industrialists, developing the copper works and a cannon- and bell-foundry into an important Boston institution. He sold his house in 1800, and moved to more elegant quarters; but the three-story North Square building remained associated with his memory, and was preserved through many years of neighborhood demolition and renewal.

The house was acquired by the Paul Revere Memorial Association in 1907, and during the next two years this group sheared off the third story and restored the building to its probable appearance in 1676. Paul Revere would have trouble recognizing his residence today, but John Jeffs and Robert Howard, and even Increase Mather, would feel right at home. It is certain, however, that old Paul would heartily approve of the museum there, which, with its old wallpaper, period furnishings, and Revere memorabilia, is one of the most interesting in Boston.

Old North Church
193 Salem Street

Like many another Boston landmark, the Old North Church bears a somewhat misleading name; in fact, it is not the Old North Church, but Christ Church, built in 1723, the oldest house of worship still standing in Boston. The Old North Church, built in 1650, stood nearby in North Square. It was destroyed by fire in 1676, was rebuilt, stood for another hundred years, and was finally pulled down by the British and used for firewood.

Christ Church was the second Episcopal church in Boston, the first being King's Chapel. Designed by the Boston printseller William Price in the manner of Sir Christopher Wren's London churches, its brick tower was surmounted by one of the architectural wonders of old Boston, a magnificent spire reaching 191 feet above the street. Dr. Timothy Cutler ministered to a congregation of wealthy and influential families, most of them connected with the royal government of the province. Many of the interior fittings were donated by philanthropic Englishmen interested in propagating the doctrines of the Church of England in Puritan Boston. Dr. Cutler voyaged to Britain in 1744 to obtain the chief ornament of the church: a marvelous chime of eight bells, inscribed with such sentiments as "We are the first ring of bells cast for the British

Old North Church

Empire in North America" and "Since generosity has opened our mouths, our tongues shall ring aloud its praise," and, of course, "God preserve the Church of England." The carillon – young Paul Revere was one of the bell-ringers – still rings out with extraordinary beauty. The King himself presented the communion plate, and a group of British Honduras merchants financed the construction of the steeple and then reserved the use of one of the handsome box pews. A certain Capt. Thomas Gruchy, a transplanted Jerseyman who commanded the privateer "Queen of Hungary," donated the trumpeting angels which grace the organ loft – booty from a French vessel taken by the "Queen."

Given the strong association with royal authority, it is ironic that the steeple of Christ Church is such a celebrated Revolutionary shrine. Robert Newman, church sexton, was a friend of Paul Revere, and permitted Capt. John Pulling to shine the lanterns on the night of April 18, 1775, thus alerting the Charlestown rebels of the British intention to cross over to their shore. Revere himself, as he rowed out on the flood tide, must have seen the double light shining out from Christ Church. Before he even touched shore, the "secret" English invasion was common knowledge, and the march on Concord doomed. And it is a further irony that General Gage, ignorant of its earlier use, chose the same steeple of Christ Church as a vantage-point from which to observe the burning of Charlestown and the British disaster at Bunker Hill. Major Pitcairn, leader of the Lexington-Concord expedition, died heroically at Bunker Hill and is buried in a vault below this church.

The steeple of Paul Revere fame came crashing down in the Great Gale of 1804, destroying an old tenement house without injuring its inhabitants. Charles Bulfinch was retained to provide a new design, in which he carefully preserved "the symmetry and proportions" of the original, although it was sixteen feet shorter. The Bulfinch steeple was itself the victim of a 1954 hurricane, and the present spire is faithful to its predecessors here at Boston's oldest house of worship.

Old North Church

Old North Church Burying Ground

Tales of a Wayside Inn

The Landlord's Tale
(Paul Revere's Ride)

Listen, my children, and you shall hear
Of the midnight ride of Paul Revere,
On the eighteenth of April, in Seventy-five;
Hardly a man is now alive
Who remembers that famous day and year.

He said to his friend, "If the British march
By land or sea from the town to-night,
Hang a lantern aloft in the belfry arch
Of the North Church tower as a signal light, –
One, if by land, and two, if by sea;
And I on the opposite shore will be,
Ready to ride and spread the alarm
Through every Middlesex village and farm,
For the country folk to be up and to arm."

Then he said, "Good night!" and with muffled oar
Silently rowed to the Charlestown shore,
Just as the moon rose over the bay,
Where swinging wide at her moorings lay
The Somerset, British man-of-war;
A phantom ship, with each mast and spar
Across the moon like a prison bar,
And a huge black hulk, that was magnified
By its own reflection in the tide.

Meanwhile, his friend, through alley and street,
Wanders and watches with eager ears,
Till in the silence around him he hears
The muster of men at the barrack door,
The sound of arms, and the tramp of feet,
And the measured tread of the grenadiers,
Marching down to their boats on the shore.

Then he climbed the tower of the Old North Church,
By the wooden stairs, with stealthy tread,
To the belfry-chamber overhead,
And startled the pigeons from their perch
On the sombre rafters, that round him made
Masses and moving shapes of shade, –
By the trembling ladder, steep and tall,
To the highest window in the wall,
Where he paused to listen and look down
A moment on the roofs of the town,
And the moonlight flowing over all.

Beneath, in the churchyard, lay the dead,
In their night-encampment on the hill,
Wrapped in silence so deep and still
That he could hear, like a sentinel's tread,
The watchful night-wind, as it went
Creeping along from tent to tent,
And seeming to whisper, "All is well!"
A moment only he feels the spell
Of the place and the hour, and the secret dread
Of the lonely belfry and the dead;
For suddenly all his thoughts are bent
On a shadowy something far away,
Where the river widens to meet the bay, –
A line of black that bends and floats
On the rising tide, like a bridge of boats.

Meanwhile, impatient to mount and ride,
Booted and spurred, with a heavy stride
On the opposite shore walked Paul Revere.
Now he patted his horse's side,
Now gazed at the landscape far and near,
Then, impetuous, stamped the earth,
And turned and tightened his saddle-girth;
But mostly he watched with eager search
The belfry-tower of the Old North Church,

As it rose above the graves on the hill,
Lonely and spectral and sombre and still.
And lo! as he looks, on the belfry's height
A glimmer, and then a gleam of light!
He springs to the saddle, the bridle he turns,
But lingers and gazes, till full on his sight
A second lamp in the belfry burns!

A hurry of hoofs in a village street,
A shape in the moonlight, a bulk in the dark,
And beneath, from the pebbles, in passing, a spark
Struck out by a steed flying fearless and fleet:
That was all! And yet, through the gloom and the light,
The fate of a nation was riding that night;
And the spark struck out by that steed, in his flight,
Kindled the land into flame with its heat.

He has left the village and mounted the steep,
And beneath him, tranquil and broad and deep,
Is the Mystic, meeting the ocean tides;
And under the alders that skirt its edge,
Now soft on the sand, now loud on the ledge,
Is heard the tramp of his steed as he rides.

It was twelve by the village clock,
When he crossed the bridge into Medford town.
He heard the crowing of the cock,
And the barking of the farmer's dog,
And felt the dap of the river fog,
That rises after the sun goes down.

It was one by the village clock,
When he galloped into Lexington.
He saw the gilded weathercock
Swim in the moonlight as he passed,
And the meeting-house windows, blank and bare,
Gaze at him with a spectral glare,
As if they already stood aghast
At the bloody work they would look upon.

It was two by the village clock,
When he came to the bridge in Concord town.
He heard the bleating of the flock,
And the twitter of birds among the trees,
And felt the breath of the morning breeze
Blowing over the meadows brown.
And one was safe and asleep in his bed
Who at the bridge would be first to fall,
Who that day would be lying dead,
Pierced by a British musket-ball.

You know the rest. In the books you have read,
How the British Regulars fired and fled, –
How the farmers gave them ball for ball,
From behind each fence and farm-yard wall,

Chasing the red-coats down the lane,
Then crossing the fields to emerge again
Under the trees at the turn of the road,
And only pausing to fire and load.

So through the night rode Paul Revere;
And so through the night went his cry of alarm
To every Middlesex village and farm, –
A cry of defiance and not of fear,
A voice in the darkness, a knock at the door,
And a word that shall echo forevermore!
For, borne on the night-wind of the Past,
Through all our history, to the last,
In the hour of darkness and peril and need,
The people will waken and listen to hear
The hurrying hoof-beats of that steed,
And the midnight message of Paul Revere.

– Henry Wadsworth Longfellow, 1863

Statue of Paul Revere

70

Paul Revere Mall

Next to Old North Church

Paul Revere Mall, the large open space linking Christ Church (known as the "Old North") and Saint Stephen's Church, is dominated by Cyrus Dallin's equestrian statue of that well-known midnight rider, Paul Revere.

In April, 1775, the Provincial Congress – by then a rebel assembly – had established itself in Lexington, a Middlesex County community whose neighbor, Concord, housed the munitions of the revolutionary army. In Boston, General Gage and his British troops were preparing to march out and capture these munitions – muskets, powder, and cannons – and it fell to Paul Revere, as official courier, to ride daily between Boston and Lexington to bring the latest intelligence to each place. On the evening of April 18, the Redcoats began to gather at Boston Common and it soon became apparent that Lexington-Concord was their destination. But how did they plan to get there?

At about eleven o'clock the light of two lanterns shone out from the steeple of Christ Church – the prearranged signal that the British would be advancing from Boston by a water route to the Charlestown shore, and then to Concord. In Boston, Revere wrapped himself in a heavy cloak, slipped down to the waterfront, and "with muffled oar, silently rowed to the Charlestown shore," passing safely by the illuminated man-o'-war *Somerset.* Landing quietly, he mounted Deacon Larkin's sturdy horse just as the moonlight revealed British transport barges rounding the point.

The rest is history, or poetry. Revere rode off through Cambridge to Medford, and from Medford to Lexington, crying out as he thundered past the sleeping farms, dismounting and pounding on doors at every village common or knot of country homes. Behind him, he left bells ringing and men shouting and dogs barking, and Minutemen pouring out of their homes to form ranks against the enemy. Other horsemen saddled up and rode off to spread the word, and by the time Revere reached Lexington the whole countryside was up in arms.

That morning, before dawn, Paul Revere was captured by an advance party of British cavalry, and detained until the troops had marched past on their way to Lexington Common. His captors had no way of knowing that the Yankee horseman had ruined their plans, and that before the sun went down that day the militia of Massachusetts – having been alerted by the cries of that selfsame horseman – would give his Majesty's troops a terrible beating in the first battle of the Revolutionary War.

Copp's Hill
Hull and Snowhill Streets

Copp's Hill was originally the North End's Windmill Hill, so-called because of a corn mill placed there in 1632. Like Beacon Hill, it was once a good deal higher, presenting an almost sheer cliff to the waterside, and sloping gradually back toward the town as a three-acre field. A fort stood here in the 1600s; and in 1659 North Burying Ground was set aside for the use of the North Enders. William Copp, an early owner of property hereabouts, was buried in the hill which bears his name.

By the time of the Revolution, several shipyards and wharves had been established at its base; and its crest commanded an excellent view of Boston and, across the Charles River, Charlestown. Here, in June, 1775, the British set up a battery which bombarded Charlestown during the Battle of Bunker Hill, setting that town ablaze. Generals Burgoyne and Clinton used it as a command post during the Battle, and were witness to the doubly awesome sight of an entire town burning to the ground and a whole army of British regulars falling dead or wounded just beyond. Even the graveyard was not immune to the horrors of that day, for errant musket balls shattered some of the stones.

Copp's Hill Burying Ground is a wonderful spot for epitaphs and old North End names: here lie the mortal remains of Messrs. Milk and Beer, and of Mistresses Brown, Scarlet and White; close by are the stones of Samuel Mower and Theodocia Hay. The illustrious

Copp's Hill Burying Ground

Here Lyes Bur
y̆ Body o

Mr SAMUEL W
Who Departed
life October 10th
Dom 1739 Ætat S

Copp's Hill Burying Ground

Mathers, for several generations the theological dictators of Boston, are here interred in the family tomb; and Edmund Hartt, the builder of the USS *Constitution*, lies within cannonshot of his creation.

In 1807 the crest of the hill was removed for use as Mill Pond landfill, and so the site of both the windmill and the British battery disappeared into the mud. For more than a decade the hill was diminished for fill, and solid blocks of buildings have sprung up where Paul Revere once cast his bells and cannons. Yet Copp's Hill endures, an irreducible element of the Boston of old.

The *Beaver*

Congress Street Bridge
Fort Point Channel

Britain's great East India Company was in trouble: it had lost vast amounts of money in supporting the war effort in India, and was determined to recoup by establishing warehouses in principal American towns, thereby undercutting American tea merchants and establishing a monopoly. But the Company didn't reckon on the intensity of opposition to this plan, both from the Sons of Liberty, who were leading a boycott against all English goods, and from the merchants, who feared the precedent of a British commodity monopoly in North America. In October, 1773 the rebellious colonies agreed among themselves to prevent the East India Company from landing and selling its tea on American shores. Then, in November, the first of three vessels – *Dartmouth, Eleanor* and *Beaver* – arrived in Boston with cargoes of Company tea.

The Royal Governor, Thomas Hutchinson, owned one of these cargoes, and insisted that it be unloaded and sold according to the provisions of the Tea Act. The other owners and almost everyone else in Boston hoped that the vessels would simply head back out to sea. Hutchinson, unmoved, double-shotted the cannon at the British fort in

Artist's rendering of the Boston Tea Party

the harbor and stationed two warships in the channel. The citizens of Boston responded by holding a mass meeting at the Old South Church on December 16, 1773.

While the British military leaders focused on the great meeting, and while Adams and Quincy harangued the assembled throng, another much smaller meeting was taking place in the back rooms of a printing shop: availing themselves of a large bowl of fish-house punch, Boston's Sons of Liberty were transforming themselves into Mohawk Indians, complete with feathers, blankets, warpaint and tomahawks. In the early evening, just as the Old South meeting broke up, these Mohawks went on the warpath, leading the crowd down to the bottom of Pearl Street, where the ships lay at Griffith's Wharf. With whoops and hollers, the eighty braves clambered aboard the three vessels and in less than three hours destroyed all 342 chests of tea, breaking open the cases and flinging them into the sea. The Redcoats never appeared; the British guns never fired; the ships were not damaged and no

one was hurt. The Tea Party had been a grand success.

Next morning, as tons of soggy East India Company tea washed ashore, Paul Revere wiped off his warpaint and set out for New York with tidings of the night's work. It was the beginning of the end for England in America, for Boston and its Mohawks had successfully defied the Crown in an act that electrified the colonies and made independence seem possible.

The Liberty Tree
Hanover Street

In the summer of 1765 all of Boston was in an uproar over the Stamp Act, a flagrant case of taxation without representation that was bitterly resented by the colonists. At daybreak on August 14, 1765, the town was startled to discover, hanging from an ancient elm tree in Hanover Square, the effigy of the royal stamp officer in Boston, Thomas Oliver. Word of the "hanging" spread, and soon thousands of people had gathered at the spot to express their admiration and approval. At dusk, the crowd took down the effigy, placed it on a funeral bier, and formed a vast procession, marching by torchlight to the stamp office, which was soon torn apart. After attacking the homes of various royal officials, the mob built a bonfire and cremated the effigy of Thomas Oliver. The next day the real Mr. Oliver was compelled to appear under the "gallows" of the Liberty Tree and renounce his duties as a stamp officer. Although chopped down by British soldiers and so re-named the Liberty Stump, the site continued to serve as a place of assembly for the patriots of Boston.

JACK FROST

80

Bunker Hill
Charlestown

The battle of Lexington-Concord on April 19, 1775 had been something of a protracted skirmish, with the Minutemen sniping at the Redcoats from behind trees and stone walls. Though badly mauled, the British still had no respect for their opponents.

On the night of June 16, 1775, the Yankee militia began to build fortifications on Breed's and Bunker Hills in Charlestown, and by daybreak they were in a position to shell Admiral Graves' men-o'-war. The British vessels immediately opened fire on the breastworks, with little initial effect. In Boston, the regulars were called out, and, under accurate covering fire, were transported to Charlestown, which was then a town in flames. As the Redcoats assembled for their first onslaught, Col. William Prescott cautioned his Minutemen not to waste their powder. "Pick off the commanders – then we'll see them run!" he said. "Don't fire until you see the color of their eyes!"

Row on row the pride of England marched up the hill, resplendent in the sun. On command, the American earthworks burst into streaks of flame and billows of white smoke: before it, the orderly red lines shuddered to a halt, and then fell back. Many English commanders lay dead on the hillside. A second attack met with the same fate. The third charge was successful in overrunning the American position, for the Yankees, having exhausted their powder, had beat a hasty retreat to safety. Though the battle had been lost, and the great patriot leader Dr. Joseph Warren lay dead, at Bunker Hill the Minutemen had proven themselves and won a great victory for the cause of freedom.

Bunker Hill Monument

USS *Constitution*
Charlestown Navy Yard

After the Revolutionary War, the American navy was disbanded, and for more than a decade no warships sailed under the stars and stripes. By 1793 our merchant vessels were being preyed upon by the Mediterranean pirates of Tripoli, and in March, 1794 Pres. Washington approved an act to build six ships for the defense of the nation.

During the summer of 1795, Edmund Hartt laid the white oak keel of a 44-gun frigate at his North End shipyard. Although peace was made that fall with the Dey of Algiers, work continued for two years on the *Constitution*. Her timbers were of white oak from New Jersey, New Hampshire and Massachusetts, live oak from the St. Simons' Islands of Georgia, and yellow pine from Georgia and the Carolinas; her white pine masts were from Maine; her copper bolts and spikes came from Paul Revere's foundry; her sails were made of nearly an acre of canvas at the Granary (the only building large enough to accommodate the work), and the Skillings brothers carved the original figurehead of Hercules presenting a scroll representing the Constitution.

After two abortive attempts, the great ship was launched on October 21, 1797. Two hundred and four feet long and 44' broad, the vessel displaced 2200 modern tons and carried 60 guns

and 400 men. Her mainmast towered 189 feet into the sky. By July, 1798, when the *Constitution* first sailed from Boston Harbor, the United States was involved in an undeclared war with France, and the ship was sent on patrol in the West Indies until a settlement was made. In 1803 she was flagship of a squadron sent to attack the persistent corsairs of Tripoli. Under Commodore Edward Preble, the *Constitution* pounded Tripoli into submission, and the Dey signed a peace treaty on shore, after a draft was initialed on the ship.

After years of increasing British harassment of American shipping, Pres. Jefferson declared an embargo on American merchant ships engaging in foreign trade; but even this unpopular measure failed, and in June, 1812, Congress declared war on England. under Capt. Isaac Hull, the *Constitution*—one of only seventeen naval vessels—engaged the 49-gun British frigate *Guerriere* off Nova Scotia in August, and within an hour the *Guerriere* had been reduced to a hulk. Having watched enemy cannonballs bounce off her stout sides, the crewmen dubbed their ship "Old Ironsides" and celebrated her first naval victory.

Capt. William Bainbridge succeeded to command, and in December, 1812, off the coast of Brazil, fell in with the 47-gun frigate *Java*. After spirited and terrible exchanges of broadsides had completely demasted the British

USS *Constitution*

USS *Constitution*

vessel and fatally wounded her commander, a lieutenant ordered her colors struck. Two years later, under Capt. Stewart, the mighty *Constitution* engaged the British ships-of-war *Cyane* and *Levant* off the coast of Portugal. Through brilliant maneuvering and deadly cannonfire, "Old Ironsides" soon made a wreck of the *Cyane. Levant* fought on, nearly escaped, but finally returned to battle and fell prize to the larger American vessel. Thus ended the fighting career of the USS *Constitution*, never beaten and never boarded.

The *Constitution* remained in Boston until 1821, when she made a cruise to the Mediterranean, returning in 1828. In response to a rumored Navy decision to scrap her, a young Harvard student named Oliver Wendell Holmes wrote a poem of protest, "Old Ironsides," which provoked such an outcry that Congress appropriated funds for her restoration. After seeing varied duty, and after several major overhauls, she was threatened with destruction as a naval target in 1905. Instead she was cosmetically restored pending a thorough rehaul in 1925. In gratitude for the American public's support, she went on a triumphal tour of 91 ports during the early 1930s.

Now berthed at the old Navy Yard in Charlestown, next to her new neighbor, the USS *Cassin Young*, the glorious *Constitution* is the oldest commissioned warship afloat in the world, the proud symbol of young America's maritime heroism.

Old Ironsides

Ay, tear her tattered ensign down!
  Long has it waved on high,
And many an eye has danced to see
  That banner in the sky;
Beneath it rung the battle shout,
  And burst the cannon's roar–
The meteor of the ocean air
  Shall sweep the clouds no more.

Her decks, once red with heroes' blood,
  Where knelt the vanquished foe,
When winds were hurrying o'er the flood,
  And waves were white below,
No more shall feel the victor's tread,
  Or know the conquered knee–
The harpies of the shore shall pluck
  The eagle of the sea!

Oh, better that her shattered hulk
  Should sink beneath the wave;
Her thunders shook the mighty deep,
  And there should be her grave;
Nail to the mast her holy flag,
  Set every threadbare sail,
And give her to the god of storms,
  The lightning and the gale!

– Oliver Wendell Holmes, 1830

Saint Stephen's Church

Hanover Street

In 1714 seventeen successful Boston artisans banded together to form a religious society which would provide spiritual sustenance to the more humble sort of citizen; and that same year they erected the New North Church building, a small wooden meeting-house in the North End, "unassisted by the more wealthy part of the community except by their prayers and good wishes." Under Rev. John Webb the society prospered; but in 1719, with the introduction of Rev. Peter Thatcher as Webb's colleague, there was a bitter and messy division within the group, a minority of which broke away to found the New Brick North Church. In 1730 the New North was enlarged, and after the Revolution the congregation was large enough to require a new and larger home.

Down came the old wooden New North, and in its place rose the new brick New North (not to be confused with the New Brick North Church), in which some of the old building's timbers were reused. As architect, the congregation wisely selected Charles Bulfinch, who provided a handsome plan somewhat similar to that of the Church of the Holy Cross (razed in 1868), the first Roman Catholic church in New England, which he had designed in 1800. The new New North featured a pilastered facade of a "bold and commanding style,"
surmounted by clock tower, belfry, and an eastern dome. Bulfinch relieved the front elevation with a Palladian window, a lunette above, and his characteristic graceful blind-arch windows. The cornerstone was laid on September 23, 1802, and the building was dedicated on May 2, 1804, having cost a total of $26,570. Rev. John Eliot and his congregation were well pleased with their new house of worship, and in the following year, for $800, purchased a bell from the foundry of Paul Revere.

Like many another congregation of this time, the New North soon turned Unitarian, and from 1813 to 1849 the Rev. Dr. Francis Parkman – father of the eminent historian – presided here. As early as the 1820s. the North End was changing so much that Dr. Parkman's flock was becoming unstable; and by the 1850s the area had become solidly Irish Catholic. In 1862 the structure was sold and became Saint Stephen's Catholic Church. Some changes were then made in the cupola; and in 1870 the whole building was moved back sixteen feet and raised six feet higher on its foundation.

By 1900 the Irish of the North End had been displaced by the Italians, whose descendants continue to worship here today. In 1964 Boston's Cardinal Cushing authorized a complete restoration of Saint Stephen's, including the reconstruction of the cupola and the lowering of the building to its original founda-

JACK FROST

tion height. In the course of this work there were some surprises, such as the discovery of the original side-entrance doors, with hardware intact, bricked up in situ. Today, Saint Stephen's stands as a wonderful example of the partnership that characterizes the city at its best: the Catholic-funded restoration and preservation of the lone Bulfinch church still standing in good old Boston.

Saint Stephen's Church

Index

Numbers in bold type indicate main listing